Needlepoint Designs after Illustrations by Beatrix Potter

Charted for Easy Use by
Rita Weiss

Dover Publications, Inc.
New York

Needlepoint Designs after Illustrations by Beatrix Potter is a new work, first published by Dover Publications, Inc. in 1976.

International Standard Book Number: 0-486-20218-6
Library of Congress Catalog Card Number: 75-9177

Manufactured in the United States of America
Dover Publications, Inc.
180 Varick Street
New York, N. Y. 10014

Introduction

Beatrix Potter, 1866-1943, the author of *The Tale of Peter Rabbit* and other popular children's books, lived in an era when needlework was one of the most popular household relaxations. A proper Victorian Englishwoman, Miss Potter would surely have learned to do needlepoint as a young girl and may have spent many hours embroidering red roses on dark backgrounds. Whether she ever thought of rendering the delightful watercolor illustrations in her books into needlepoint we will never know, but surely a more desirable marriage could not be arranged.

This collection of twenty-four charted designs is adapted from my four favorite Beatrix Potter books, *The Tale of Peter Rabbit* (illustrations 1-8), *The Tale of Benjamin Bunny* (9-12), *The Tailor of Gloucester* (13-19), and *The Tale of Two Bad Mice* (20-24).

Although the designs are charted for working on a #12 needlepoint canvas, they can be executed on other types of canvas, and can also be used for other crafts. If you prefer working on a #10 canvas, the designs will be proportionately larger; on #14, proportionately smaller. To make a Beatrix Potter rug, work any of the designs on a #5 or #4 canvas, which will make them larger. You can also use these charted patterns in cross-stitch embroidery or for Fair Isle knitting. You can work each design as a complete picture or combine elements and characters from several designs for a Beatrix Potter needlepoint montage.

Before beginning any project, you should work out a complete, detailed color scheme for the design. You will find it convenient to put tracing paper over the designs in the book and to experiment with colors on the tracing paper. In this way the design in the book will not be ruined if you decide to change colors. The photographs of the finished needlepoint may suggest some color combinations. You might also want to look at the actual watercolor illustrations in Miss Potter's books, all of which are available as inexpensive Dover reprints. I have worked the designs in the soft, pastel colors that Beatrix Potter used in her illustrations. There is no reason, however, why you cannot be more adventurous in your choice of colors if you wish.

After you have worked out a suitable color scheme, you can work the design directly onto the canvas by counting out the number of warp and woof squares shown in the diagram, each square on the chart representing one stitch to be taken on the canvas. If you have always worked your designs on pre-painted canvases, you will find working a design from a chart is fun and challenging. There is something very exciting about seeing a figure gradually emerge from a completely blank canvas. If this is your first attempt at working from a chart, you may want to begin with one of the fairly easy designs which have only one figure represented.

You may prefer to outline your design on the canvas itself. Since needlepoint canvas is almost transparent, it can be placed over any design in this book, and then the pattern can be traced directly onto the #12 canvas. If you decide to paint the entire design onto the canvas make sure your medium is waterproof! Use either a nonsoluble ink, acrylic paint thinned appropriately with water so as not to clog the holes in the canvas, or oil paint mixed with benzine or turpentine. Felt-tip pens are also very handy both for outlining and coloring in the design on the canvas, but check the labels carefully because not all felt markers are waterproof. Allow all paint to dry thoroughly before beginning the project.

There are two distinct types of needlepoint canvas: single-mesh and double-mesh. Double-mesh is woven with two horizontal and two vertical threads forming each mesh, whereas single-mesh is woven with one vertical and one horizontal thread forming each mesh. Double-mesh is a very stable canvas on which the threads will stay securely in place as you work. Single-mesh canvas, which is more widely used today, is a little easier on the eyes because the spaces are slightly larger. The finished needlepoint pictured in this book was all done on single-mesh canvas.

A tapestry needle with a rounded, blunt tip and an elongated eye is used for needlepoint. Needles range in size from #24 to #13; the smaller the number, the larger the needle. The correct needle size is determined by the size canvas you are using. The needle should clear the holes in the canvas without spreading the threads. A #18 needle is commonly used for a #10 canvas, while either a # 18 or #20 is used for a #12 canvas. Special yarns which have good twist and are sufficiently heavy to cover the canvas are used for needlepoint. Tapestry yarn, a 3-ply, tightly twisted yarn, was the original needlepoint yarn. While it is today being dyed in bright, modern colors, it is still generally available only in the more traditional colors. Persian type yarn is a 3-ply yarn, lightly twisted together, that can be separated for use on different types of canvas. Persian yarn is available in a wide range of colors and has a sheen that adds a certain luxuriousness to the completed project. All of the needlepoint shown in this book was rendered with Persian yarn. The best way to determine the amount of yarn you need is to work a square inch in the type of stitch and with the materials you are planning to use. You can then estimate the amount of yarn needed by multiplying the amount of yarn used in the sample by the number of square inches in that particular color. Most needlepoint shops can estimate the amount of yarn needed for a particular project with almost uncanny accuracy. Remember that a needlepoint project takes a great deal of time to complete but that the finished work can last indefinitely. It is foolish economy to use cheap materials that will not reflect the amount of labor you have put into a project.

When starting a project, allow at least a 2″ margin of plain canvas around the needlepoint design. Bind all of the edges with masking tape; needlepoint canvas is sharp, and the binding will not only keep your threads from snagging but will save your fingers from unnecessary cuts. Generally it is best to begin working close to the center and work outward toward the edges of the canvas, working the backgrounds or borders last. To avoid fraying your yarn, work with strands not longer than 18".

The Tent Stich is universally considered to be *the* needlepoint stitch. The three most familiar versions of Tent Stitch are: Plain Half-Cross Stitch, Continental Stitch and Basket Weave Stitch. The use to which you are planning to put your finished project has a great deal to do with your choice of stitch.

Plain Half-Cross Stitch, while the most economical in the use of yarn (it uses about 1 yard per square inch of canvas) is not very durable and should only be used for projects which will have little wear, such as pictures or wall hangings. It also has a tendency to pull the needlepoint out of shape, a disadvantage that can be corrected by blocking.

Continental Stitch uses slightly more yarn (about 1¼ yards per square inch), but it is more durable since the stitch works up with more thickness on the back than on the front. This is an ideal stitch for projects which will receive a great deal of wear, such as pillows, belts, purses and upholstery. The Continental Stitch also tends to pull the canvas out of shape.

The Basket Weave Stitch, which makes a very well padded and durable article, requires the same amount of yarn as the Continental Stitch, does not pull the canvas out of shape, and works up very quickly because there is no need to keep turning the canvas. It does lack maneuverability, however, and is awkward to work in areas where small shapes or intricate designs are planned. It is, however, an excellent stitch to use for large areas or backgrounds.

PLAIN HALF-CROSS STITCH: Always work Half-Cross Stitch from left to

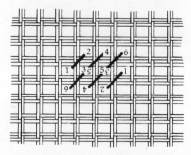

right, then turn the canvas around and work the return row, still stitching from left to right. Bring the needle to the front of the canvas at a point that will be the bottom of the first stitch. The needle is in a vertical position when making the stitch. Keep the stitches loose for minimum distortion and good coverage. This stitch must be worked on a double-mesh canvas.

CONTINENTAL STITCH: Start this design at the upper right-hand corner

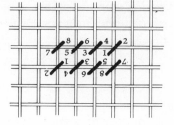

and work from right to left. The needle is slanted and always brought out a mesh ahead. The resulting stitch is actually a Half-Cross Stitch on top and a slanting stitch on the back. When the row is finished, turn the canvas around and work the return row, still stitching from right to left.

BASKET WEAVE STITCH: Start the Basket Weave in the top right-hand

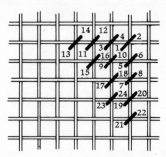

corner. Work the rows diagonally, first going down the canvas from left to right and then up the canvas from right to left. The rows must be alternated properly or a faint ridge will show where the pattern has been interrupted. Always stop working in the middle of a row rather than the end so that you will know in which direction you are working.

The finished needlepoint pictured in this book was all rendered in Tent Stitch for consistency. There are, however, hundreds of different needlepoint stitches. Many of these stitches used either as backgrounds or for accents can add a great deal to your finished work. When you work a background in Brick or Mosaic Stitch, the design done in Tent Stitch will stand out in relief. A dress or suit worked in Scotch or Checker Stitch will look like a textured fabric. When using an accent stitch, it is easier to do the parts of the canvas that are to be rendered in Tent Stitch first, and then to fill in the remaining area with the accent stitch. There will be some areas where the entire sequence of accent stitches will not fit. In these places it will be necessary to use only the portion that fits while still maintaining the general pattern. Some of the stitches which you may find fun to use are:

MOSAIC STITCH: This is a very practical background stitch to use in con-

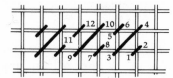

junction with Tent Stitch because it creates texture without overpowering the design.

CASHMERE STITCH: Like the Mosaic, this makes a nice background because of its small, neat pattern.

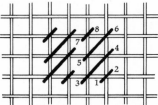

SCOTCH STITCH: The group of five stitches of different lengths in a square

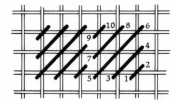

forms a pattern. Once you have worked the first row, the pattern falls into place.

CHECKER STITCH: This is actually the Scotch Stitch used in conjunction with Tent Stitch to form a checker pattern. You can work this in two colors to give a plaid-like effect.

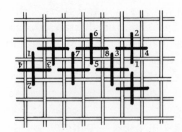

UPRIGHT CROSS STITCH: This stitch gives a very interesting, firm texture. You must complete each cross before going on to the next one. In order to give the finished design a neat look, make certain that all stitches cross in the same direction.

BRICK STITCH: The stitches, executed in upright rows, are set in alternating rows to form a brick design. Stitches should be worked with a loose, even tension in order to cover the canvas. Although the diagram shows the stitches worked over four threads for ease in following, this stitch should be worked over only two threads when used in conjunction with Tent Stitch so as not to overpower the design.

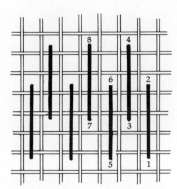

When you have finished your needlepoint, it should be blocked. No matter how straight you have kept your work, blocking will give it a professional look.

Any hard, flat surface that you do not mind marring with nail holes and one that will not be warped by wet needlepoint can serve as a blocking board. A large piece of plywood, an old drawing board or an old-fashioned doily blocker is ideal.

Moisten a Turkish towel in cold water and roll the needlepoint in the towel. Leaving the needlepoint in the towel overnight will insure that both the canvas and the yarn are thoroughly and evenly dampened. Do not saturate the needlepoint! Never hold the needlepoint under the faucet as this much water is not necessary.

Mark the desired outline on the blocking board, making sure that the corners are straight. Lay the needlepoint on the blocking board, and tack the canvas with thumbtacks about ½" to ¾" apart. It will probably take a good deal of pulling and tugging to get the needlepoint straight, but do not be afraid of this stress. Leave the canvas on the blocking board until thoroughly dry. Never put an iron on your needlepoint. You cannot successfully block with a steam iron because the needlepoint must dry in the straightened position. You may also have needlepoint blocked professionally. If you have a pillow made, a picture framed, or a chair seat mounted, the craftsman may include the blocking in his price.

Your local needlepoint shop or department where you buy your materials will be happy to help you with any problems.

I should personally like to thank Frank Fontana for his painstaking work in helping to prepare the charts; Dolly Carrello and James Spero for their help in adapting some of Beatrix Potter's original designs; Linda Egbert, Bella Moltz and Sabrina Weiss for their help in rendering some of the backgrounds; my husband and family for living with yarn in their soup, and Beatrix Potter for creating her delightful animal friends.

1 "Now my dears," said Mrs. Rabbit, "you may go into the fields or down the
lane, but don't go into Mr. McGregor's garden."

—*The Tale of Peter Rabbit*

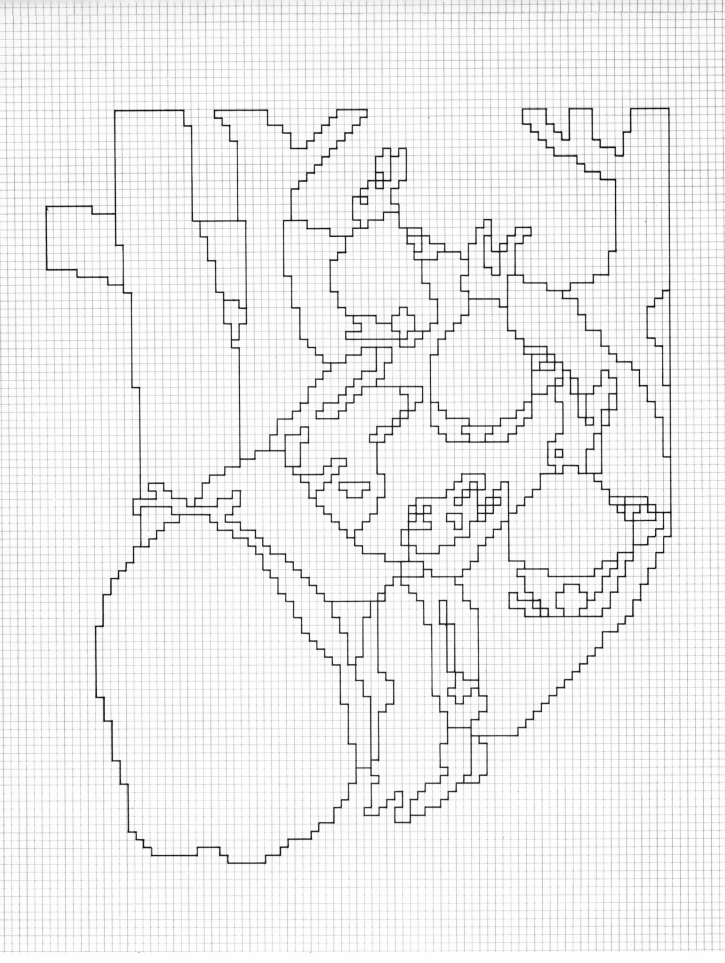

2 "Now run along, and don't get into mischief. I am going out."
—*The Tale of Peter Rabbit*

3 Then old Mrs. Rabbit took a basket and her umbrella, and went through the wood to the baker's.

—*The Tale of Peter Rabbit*

4 Flopsy, Mopsy and Cotton-tail, who were good little bunnies, went down the lane to gather blackberries.

—*The Tale of Peter Rabbit*

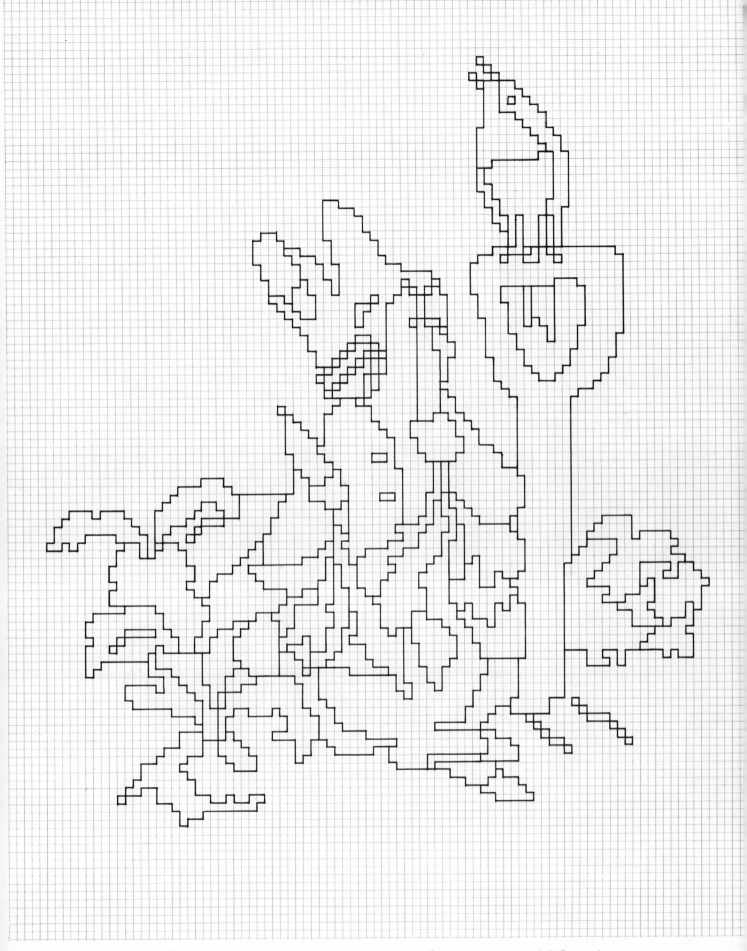

5 But Peter, who was very naughty, ran straight away to Mr. McGregor's garden. First, he ate some lettuces and some French beans.

—*The Tale of Peter Rabbit*

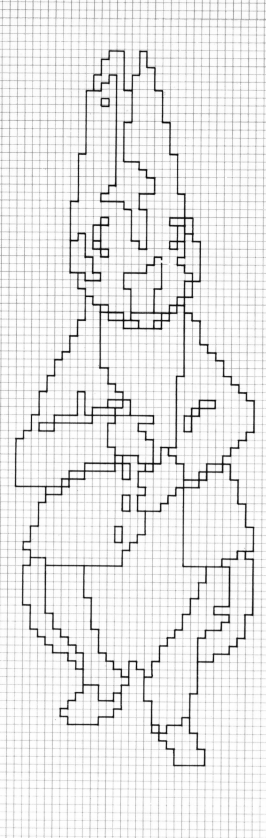

6 And then, feeling rather sick, he went to look for some parsley.
—*The Tale of Peter Rabbit*

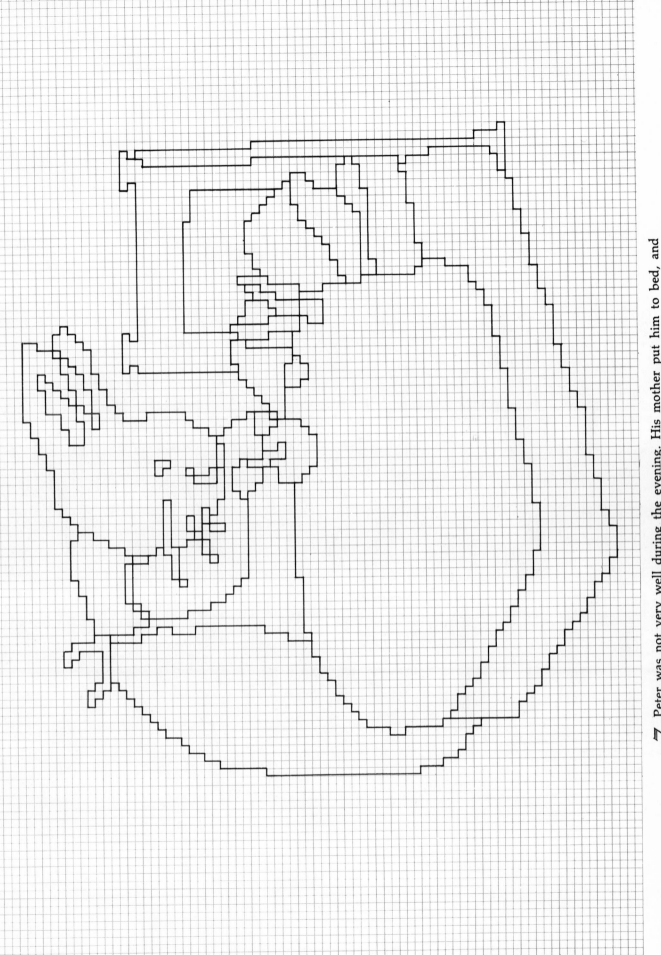

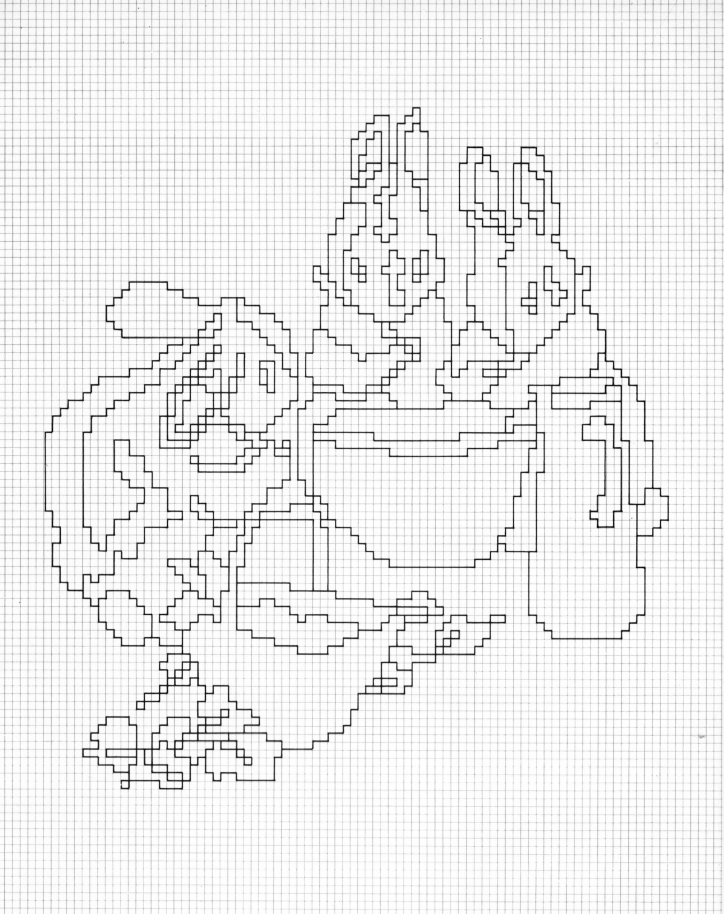

8 But Flopsy, Mopsy and Cotton-tail had bread and milk and blackberries for supper.

—The Tale of Peter Rabbit

9 Little Benjamin sat down beside his cousin and assured him.
—*The Tale of Benjamin Bunny*

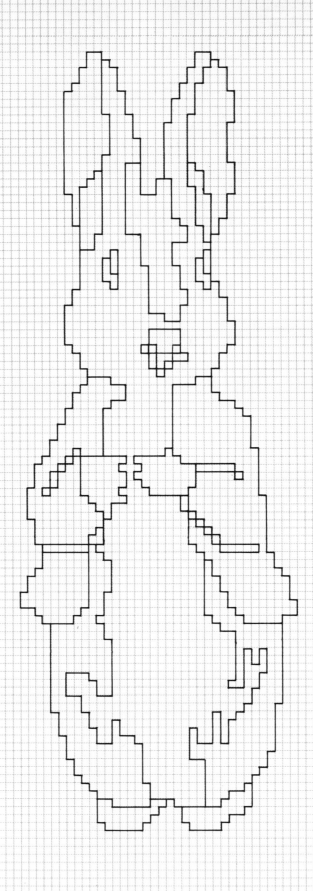

10 Peter did not seem to be enjoying himself; he kept hearing noises.
—*The Tale of Benjamin Bunny*

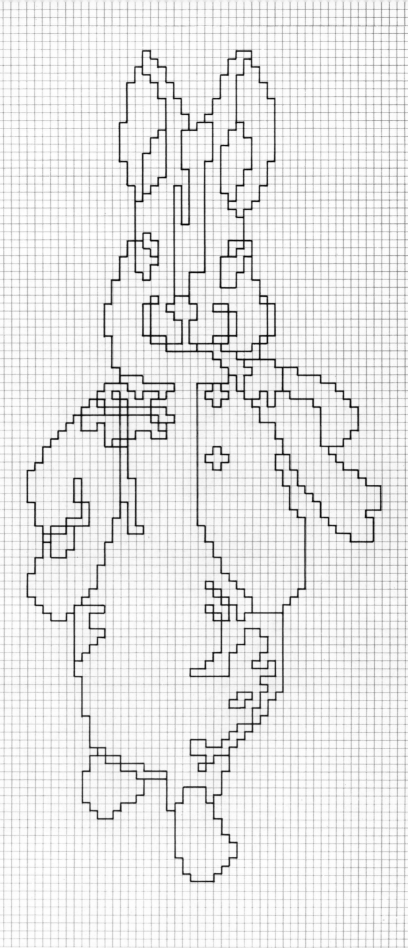

11   Benjamin, on the contrary, was perfectly at home, and ate a lettuce leaf.
—*The Tale of Benjamin Bunny*

12 Benjamin tried on the tam-o'-shanter, but it was too big for him.
　　　　　　　　　　　　　—The Tale of Benjamin Bunny

13 In the time of swords and periwigs, there lived a tailor in Gloucester.
—*The Tailor of Gloucester*

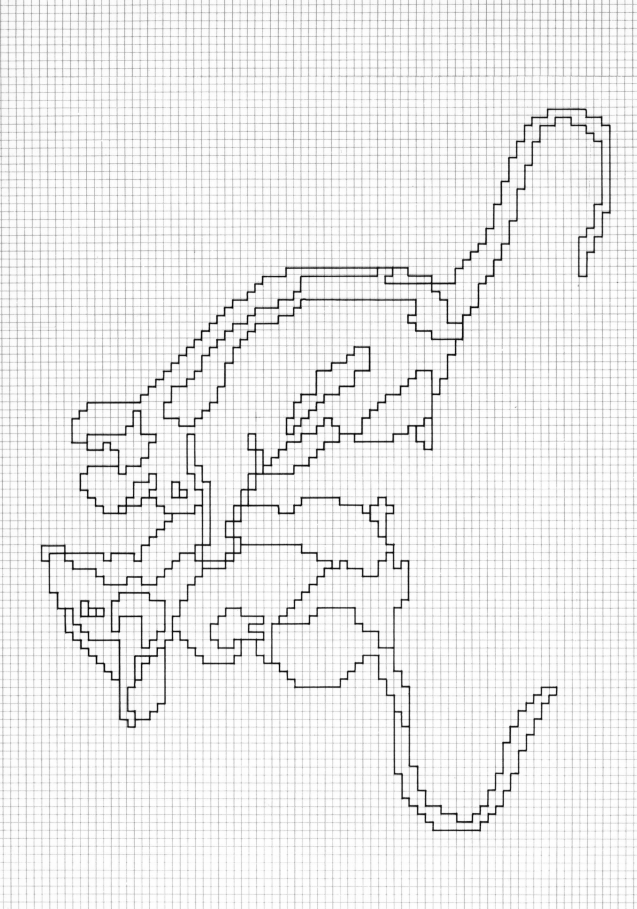

14 He cut his coats without waste, and there were very small ends and snippets —"Too narrow breadths for nought—except waistcoats for mice," said the tailor.

—*The Tailor of Gloucester*

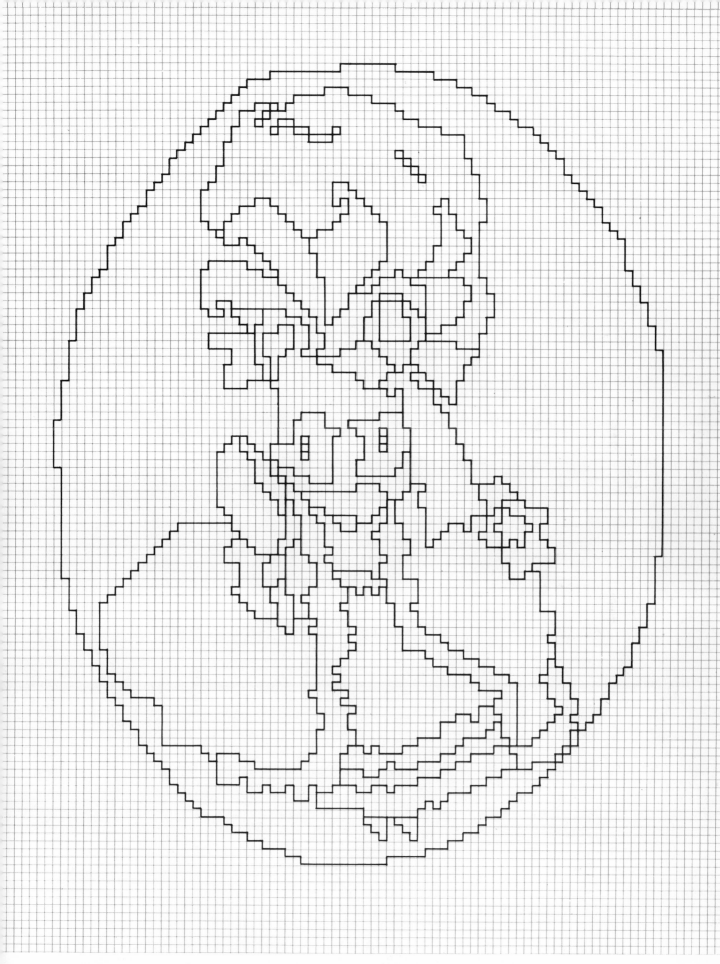

15 'No breadth at all; tippets for mice and ribbons for mobs! for mice!"
—*The Tailor of Gloucester*

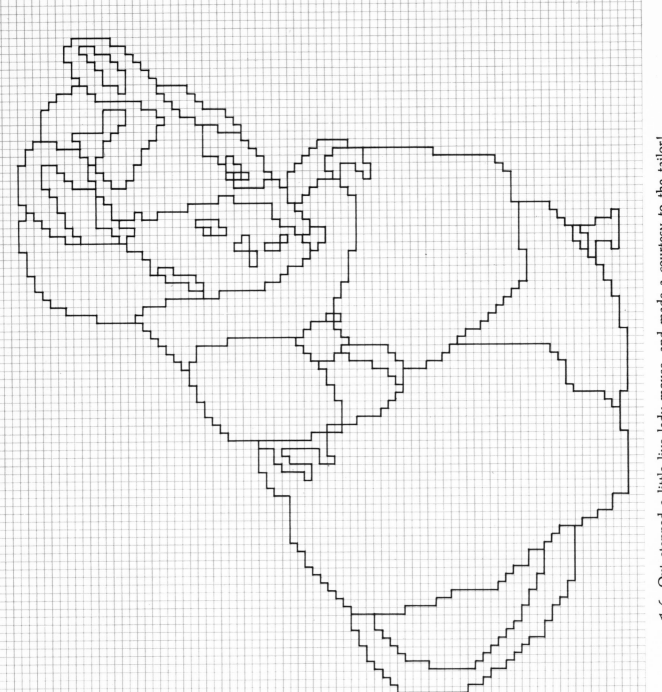

16 Out stepped a little live lady mouse, and made a courtesy to the tailor!
—*The Tailor of Gloucester*

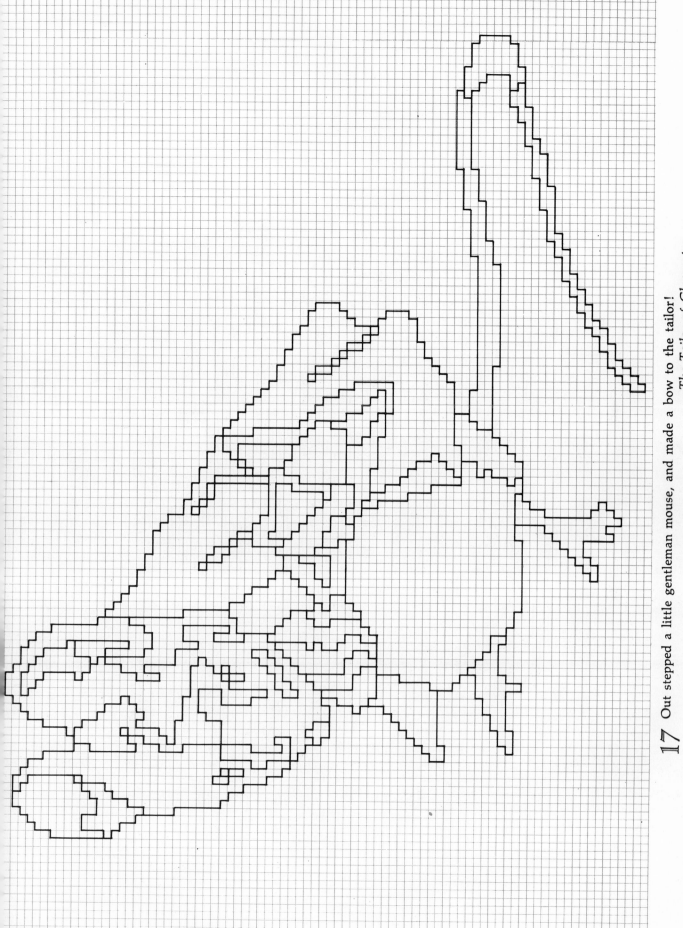

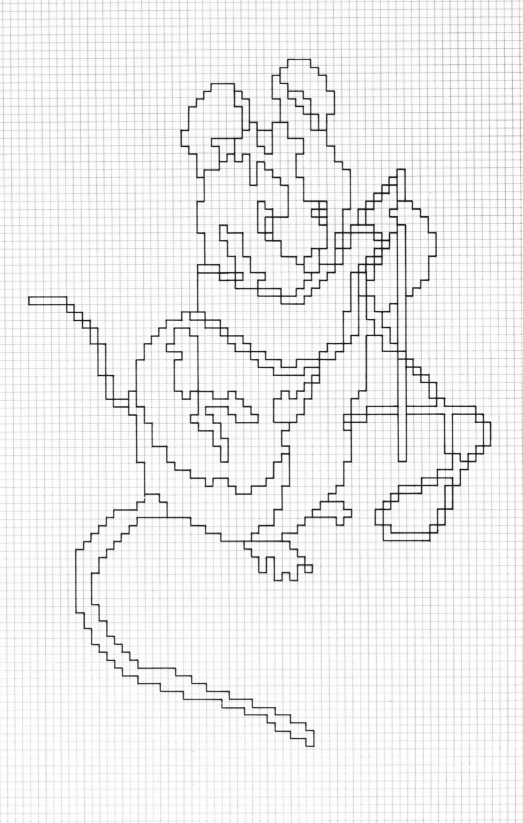

18 Who should come to sew when the window was barred, and the door was fast locked?

—*The Tailor of Gloucester*

19 There was a snippeting of scissors, and snappeting of thread; and little mouse voices sang loudly and gaily.

—*The Tailor of Gloucester*

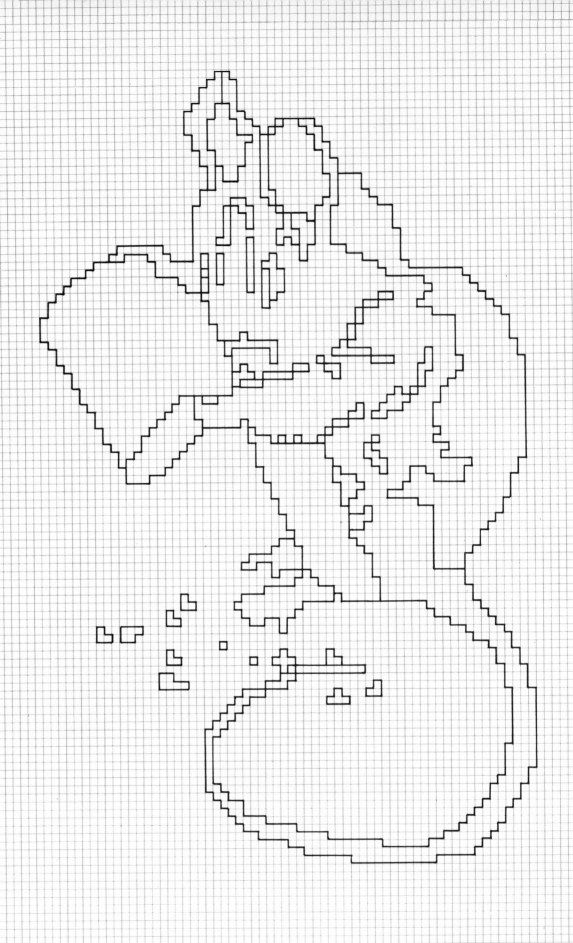

20 Hunca Munca found some tiny canisters; but when she turned them upside down there was nothing inside except red beads.

—The Tale of Two Bad Mice

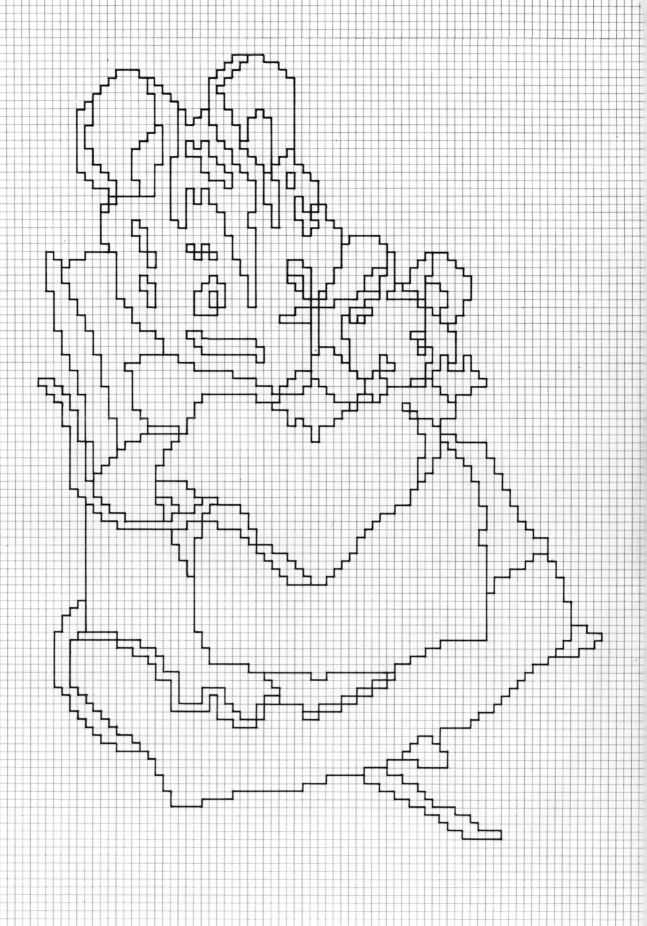

21 Hunca Munca has the cradle and some of Lucinda's clothes.
   —*The Tale of Two Bad Mice*

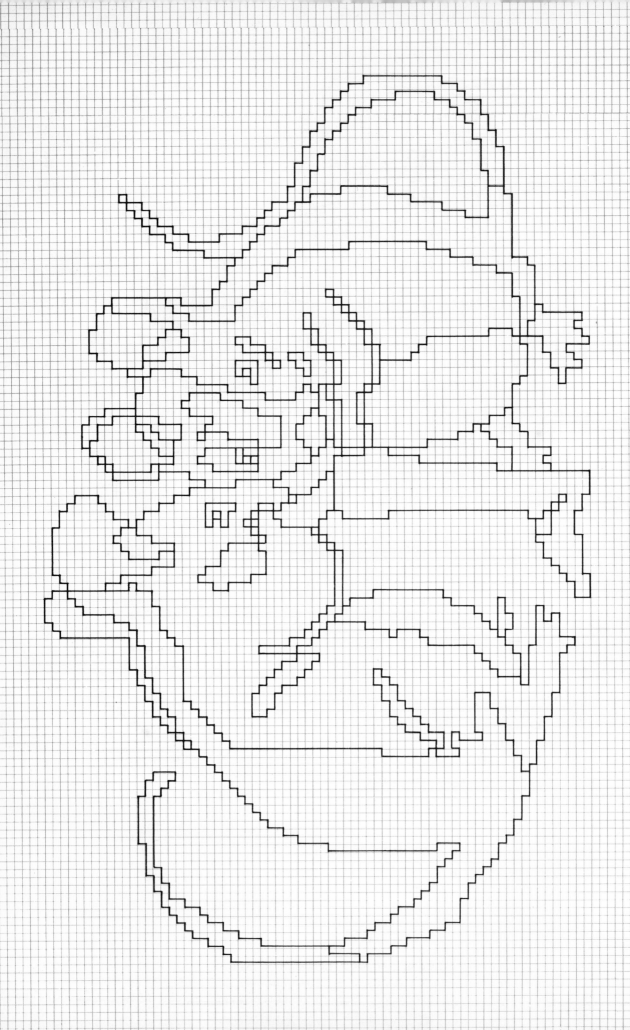

Tom Thumb found a crooked sixpence; and upon Christmas Eve he and Hunca Munca stuffed it into one of the stockings.

—*The Tale of Two Bad Mice*

23 And very early every morning—before anybody is awake—Hunca Munca
comes with the dust pan and her broom—

—*The Tale of Two Bad Mice*

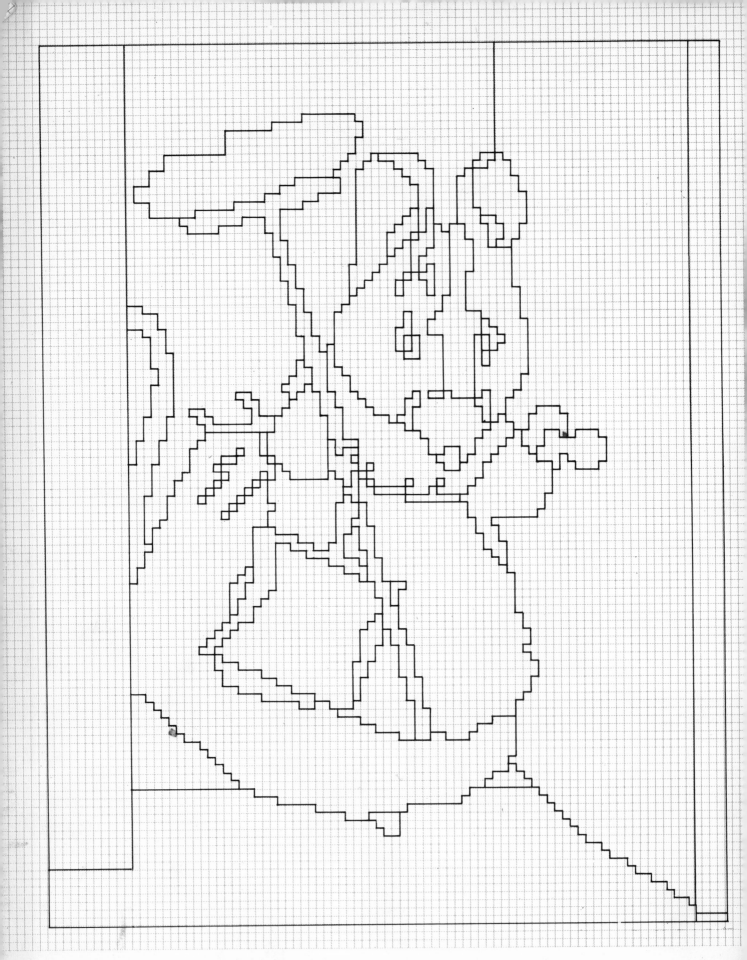

24   —to sweep the Dollies' house!

—*The Tale of Two Bad Mice*